WHEN I WAS EIGHT

Christy Jordan-Fenton & Margaret Pokiak-Fenton
Art by Gabrielle Grimard

annick press
toronto + berkeley

The school Margaret
attended in Aklavik

I knew many things when I was eight. I knew how to keep the sled dogs quiet while Father snuck up on caribou, and to bring the team to him after a kill. I knew the sun slept in the winter and woke in the summer.

And I knew that when the sun-warmed Arctic Ocean shrugged off its slumbering ice, we would cross it to trade furs with the outsiders.

But I did not know how to read the outsiders' books.
It was not enough to hear them from my older sister,
Rosie. I longed to read them for myself.

Although I begged like a hungry dog after scraps, Father
would not let me go to the outsiders' school, like Rosie.
He knew things about the school that I did not. But my
name is Olemaun (that's *OO-lee-maun*), the stubborn
stone that sharpens the half-moon ulu knife used by
our women.

I wore away at him all through the winter. And when the sun awoke again and we traveled to trade with the outsiders, he reluctantly left me at their school.

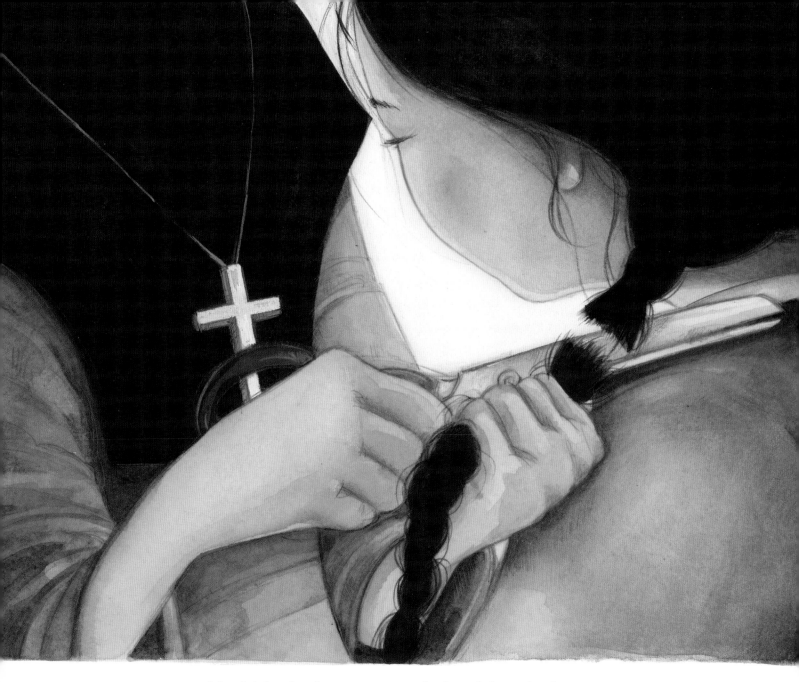

A black-cloaked nun cut my hair. I felt naked as my braids fell to the floor. Stripped of my warm parka, I was made to wear a thin pinafore and scratchy underwear, with stockings too small to stay above my knees.

My Inuit name was taken and I was to be called Margaret.
All I had left was a beautiful book my sister read me about
a girl named Alice. I hugged it to my chest and tried to be
brave like the girl in the story.

Every day for weeks, we woke very early for chores.
Instead of sitting in desks, we scrubbed the floor beneath
them. We washed walls and dishes and laundry, and then
we went to church and kneeled on our already aching
knees to clean our souls. I worked hard, but it brought
me no closer to being able to read.

When the first skiff of snow returned and my hopes were nearly dead, the kindly head nun led us to a classroom and told us to be seated. At last, we were going to read!

Behind the teacher's desk sat the nun who had cut my hair. I didn't want her for a teacher, but I sat very tall so she would know I was eager. A few older girls raised their hands, so I did, too. The nun laughed and motioned for me to stand and read. Read? I couldn't even speak English. I scowled at her as the others giggled. Instead of learning to read that day, I spent the rest of the class with my nose in the corner and my stockings slouched around my ankles.

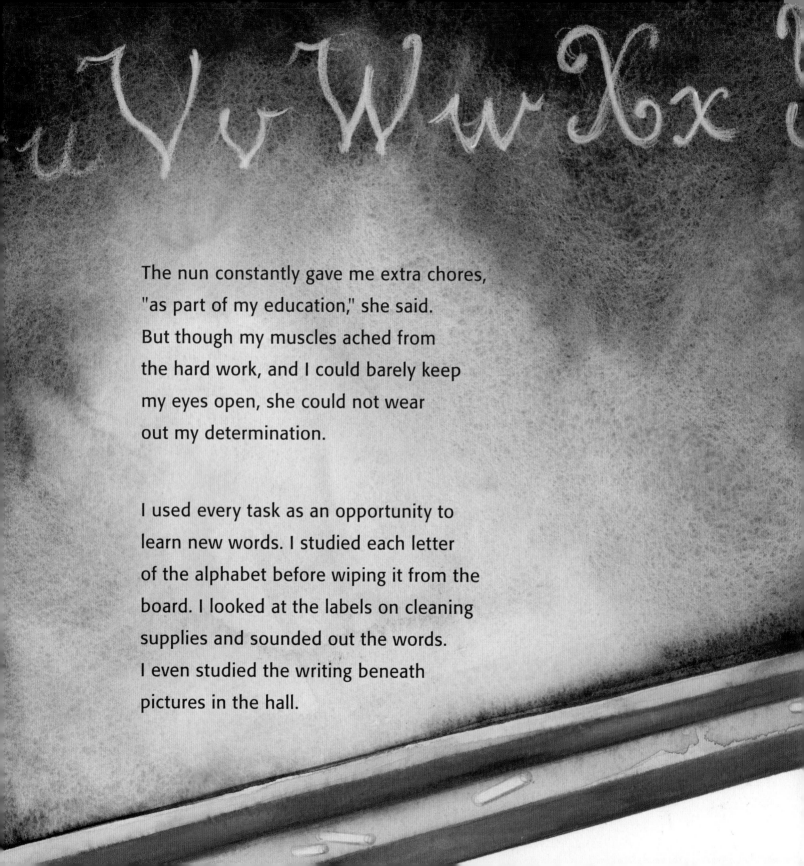

The nun constantly gave me extra chores,
"as part of my education," she said.
But though my muscles ached from
the hard work, and I could barely keep
my eyes open, she could not wear
out my determination.

I used every task as an opportunity to
learn new words. I studied each letter
of the alphabet before wiping it from the
board. I looked at the labels on cleaning
supplies and sounded out the words.
I even studied the writing beneath
pictures in the hall.

These things improved my reading, but I longed to read an actual book— my book.

One evening, I hurried through my supper of cabbage soup, planning a hasty escape. I couldn't wait anymore. I dashed into the hall, but the nun was waiting for me.

"Not so fast, Margaret. There are pots to be scrubbed," she said in a threatening tone, and marched me to the kitchen.

With my arms in scalding water up to my elbows I couldn't hold back my frustration. "I could be reading," I muttered.

"What?" the nun demanded, her shoes creaking as she crossed the kitchen. She pinned me against the sink. Slowly, a smile spread across her thin lips. "Fetch me a cabbage from the basement," she ordered.

I'd heard stories of children who disappeared down in that dark cavern.

I descended each step deliberately, hiding my fear. My hands quickly found a cabbage in the shadows and I scurried up the stairs. But she slammed the door, shutting out all light.

I pulled the handle. It was locked.
A scream built in my chest, but I held it in.
I closed my eyes, pulled up my stockings, and
breathed deeply, until I could feel my father's
presence. He wrapped his arms around me in
the darkness and I spelled out my Inuit name
to him, whispering, O - L - E - M - A - U - N .
His proud smile made me stronger, so I worked
through the name of my distant home,
B - A - N - K - S - I - S - L - A - N - D.

I spelled many things from home and was
starting on the title of my book—A - L - I —
when the door opened. I squeezed past the
nun and returned to the sink. Her angry black
eyes raised goose bumps on the back of my
shaved neck, but she could not make me cry.

When I returned to the dorm room that night, all the girls
were giddy. Everyone had beautiful new dark stockings!
I pulled off my old ones, took my place in front of the nun,
held out my hands, and closed my eyes.

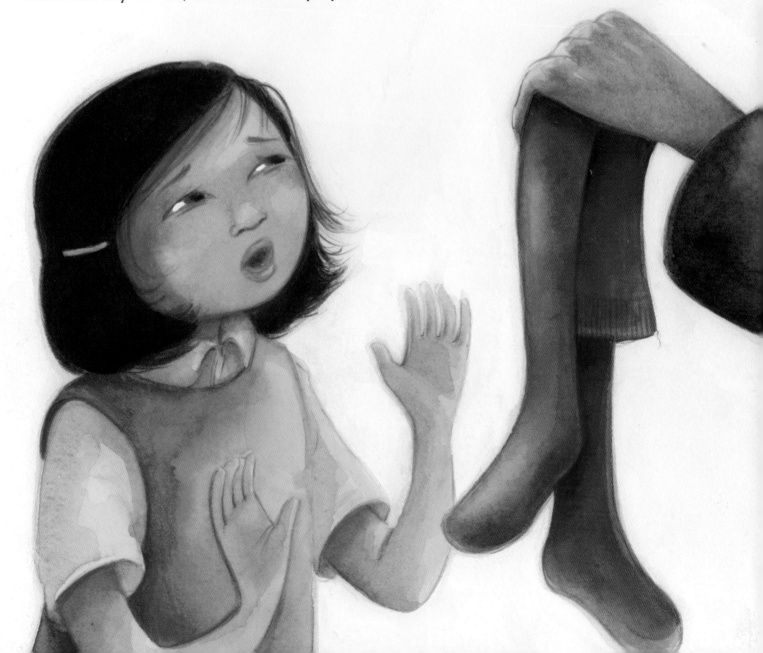

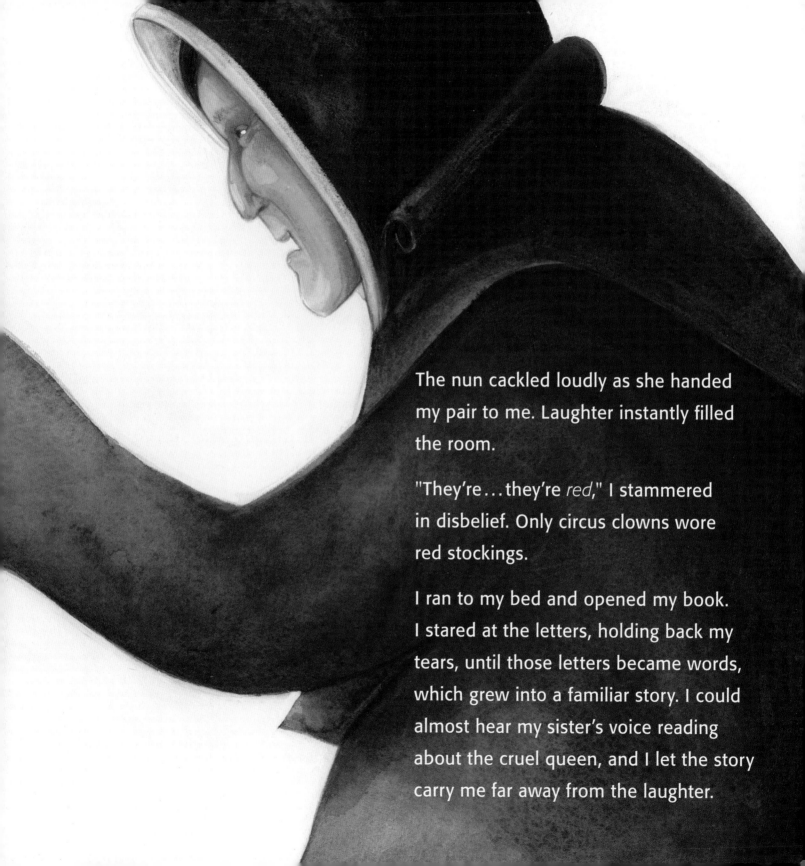

The nun cackled loudly as she handed my pair to me. Laughter instantly filled the room.

"They're...they're *red*," I stammered in disbelief. Only circus clowns wore red stockings.

I ran to my bed and opened my book. I stared at the letters, holding back my tears, until those letters became words, which grew into a familiar story. I could almost hear my sister's voice reading about the cruel queen, and I let the story carry me far away from the laughter.

The next morning I crept quietly to breakfast. But an older girl saw me and called out, "Fatty Legs!" as bits of food fell from her mouth.

"Fatty Face!" I shouted back. "F-A-T-T—"

The nun swooped in. "If you cannot get along with the others, you can tend to the laundry," she hissed.

I entered the laundry and stood beside the large vat with the fire crackling beneath it. And then the idea came to me. I knew what to do with my stockings.

I burned them to ashes. I felt like Alice after a bite of magic cake— as large as the entire room.

When the nun saw my bare legs, she exploded.
"Margaret! Put on your stockings!" she demanded.

I set my jaw and crossed my arms. "I can't."

"Why not?"

"I just can't."

Her face grew very red and she ordered everyone to
search the room. Like the Queen's henchmen in my
book, they scurried around, upturning everything.
Books were torn from shelves and blankets from beds.
No one was calling me Fatty Legs now. And no amount
of searching could ever bring those stockings back.

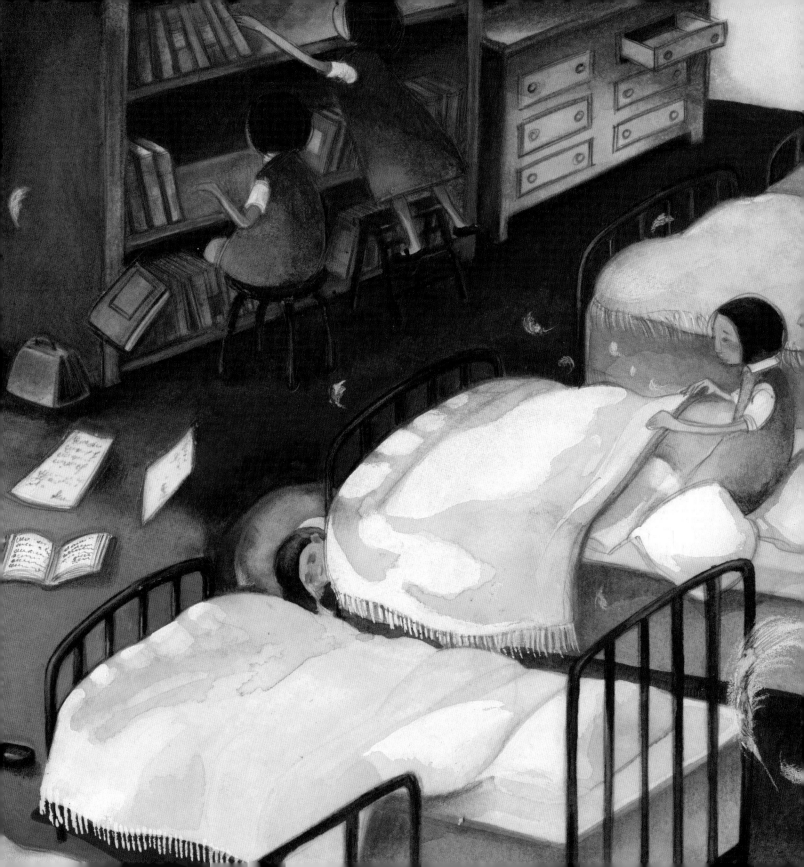

The nun snarled when I was allowed another pair. In my
new thick, gray stockings I felt victorious. But when I strode
into class the next day, the nun slammed a book on my desk.
It was a green reader, like the older girls used.

"Page thirty-four," she said.

She wanted to cut me down to size.

I opened the book, nervousness swelling
in my throat. I looked at the words
and began slowly, twisting my tongue
around the consonants and forming my
mouth around the vowels.

By the second paragraph, I confidently
sliced through the words without a
single moment of hesitation.

There was no stopping me.

When I finished, I looked up, but the nun was facing the blackboard.

"Sit down, Margaret," she said.

I felt a great happiness inside that I dared not show.
I quietly took my seat. I was Olemaun, conqueror of evil,
reader of books. I was a girl who traveled to a strange
and faraway land to stand against a tyrant, like Alice.
And like Alice, I was brave, clever, and as unyielding
as the strong stone that sharpens an ulu.

I finally knew this,
like I knew many things,
because now I could read.

Dedication

For my three little inspirations: You color my world and nurture my imagination in so many vibrant ways. For Justice Murray Sinclair and his beautiful wife, Katherine: I am in awe of the ways you answer the call of the people so selflessly. May the Creator always be with you to give you strength for the good work you do. *Wiidookawishin ji wiidookaawigwaa niij Anishinaabegm*
—Christy

For the Indian Residential School survivors who haven't yet found their voices
—Margaret

For all the little Olemauns of the world
—Gabrielle

© 2013 Christy Jordan-Fenton and Margaret Pokiak-Fenton (text)
© 2013 Gabrielle Grimard (illustrations)
Eleventh printing, June 2020
Edited by Debbie Rogosin
Designed by Natalie Olsen/Kisscut Design
Title page image © Fleming/NWT Archives/N-1979-050-0042

Annick Press Ltd.

We acknowledge the support of the Canada Council for the Arts, the Ontario Arts Council, and the participation of the Government of Canada/la participation du gouvernement du Canada for our publishing activities.

Cataloging in Publication

Jordan-Fenton, Christy
When I was eight / Christy Jordan-Fenton and Margaret Pokiak-Fenton ; art by Gabrielle Grimard.

Adaption of: Fatty legs.
Issued also in electronic format.
ISBN 978-1-55451-491-5 (bound).—ISBN 978-1-55451-490-8 (pbk.)

1. Pokiak-Fenton, Margaret—Childhood and youth—Juvenile literature.   2. Inuit—Canada—Residential schools—Juvenile literature.   3. Inuit women—Biography—Juvenile literature.   I. Pokiak-Fenton, Margaret   II. Grimard, Gabrielle, 1975–   III. Title.   IV. Title: Fatty legs.

E96.5.J653 2013   j371.829'9712071   C2012-906193-X

Published in the U.S.A. by Annick Press (U.S.) Ltd.
Distributed in Canada by University of Toronto Press.
Distributed in the U.S.A. by Publishers Group West.

Printed in China

Visit us at: www.annickpress.com